Online Bullying

Addy Ferguson

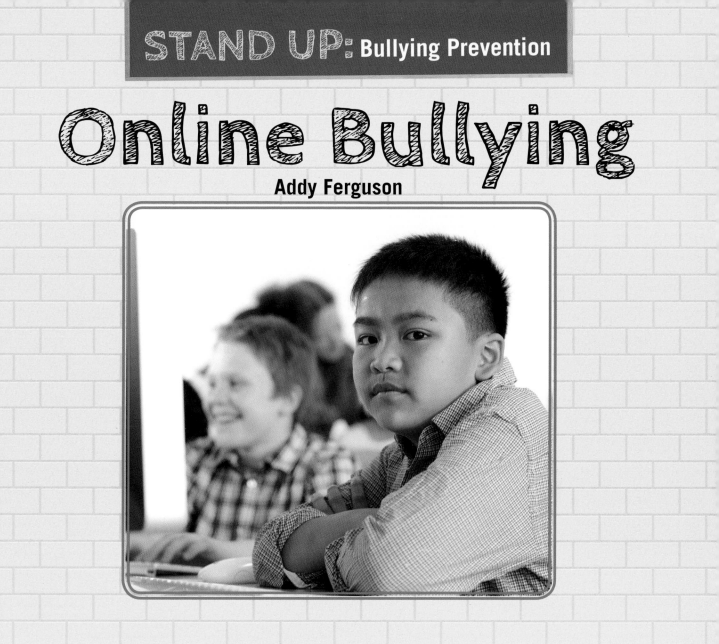

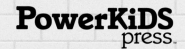
New York

Published in 2013 by The Rosen Publishing Group, Inc.
29 East 21st Street, New York, NY 10010

First Edition

Editor: Jennifer Way
Book Design: Erica Clendening and Colleen Bialecki

Photo Credits: Cover David Leahy/Digital Vision/Getty Images; p. 4 © iStockphoto.com/1MoreCreative; p. 5 Jupiterimages/liquidlbrary/Thinkstock; p. 6 Hemera/Thinkstock; p. 7 Peter Dazeley/StockImage/Getty Images; p. 8 KidStock/Blend Images/Getty Images; pp. 9, 10 iStockphoto/Thinkstock; p. 11 Michael Krasowitz/Photographer's Choice/Getty Images; p. 13 Blend Images/Ariel Skelley/the Agency Collection/Getty Images; p. 14 © iStockphoto.com/Digitalskillet; p. 15 Glow Images, Inc/Getty Images; p. 16 Will and Deni McIntyre/Photo Researchers/Getty Images; p. 17 © iStockphoto.com/Grady Reese; p. 18 Yellow Dog Productions/The Image Bank/Getty Images; p. 19 Steve Debenport/The Agency Collection/Getty Images; p. 20 Echo/Cultura/Getty Images; p. 21 Bob Winsett/Photolibrary/Getty Images; p. 22 Jose Luis Pelaez/Iconica/Getty Images.

Library of Congress Cataloging-in-Publication Data

Ferguson, Addy.
 Online bullying / by Addy Ferguson. — 1st ed.
    p. cm. — (Stand up: bullying prevention)
 Includes index.
 ISBN 978-1-4488-9668-4 (library binding) — ISBN 978-1-4488-9794-0 (pbk.) —
 ISBN 978-1-4488-9795-7 (6-pack)
 1. Cyberbullying—Juvenile literature. 2. Cyberbullying—Prevention—Juvenile literature.
 3. Bullying—Prevention—Juvenile literature. I. Title.
 HV6773.15.C92F47 2013
 302.34'302854678—dc23
                                      2012025151

Manufactured in the United States of America

CPSIA Compliance Information: Batch #W13PK4: For Further Information contact Rosen Publishing, New York, New York at 1-800-237-9932

Contents

What Is Bullying?

Do you know what bullying is? Bullying is when one person targets another person and **taunts**, **humiliates,** threatens, embarrasses, or harasses him in some way. There is more than one kind of bully, though.

Verbal bullies might taunt their victims or call them cruel names.

Physical bullies push around, beat up, or threaten to hurt their victims.

There are **verbal bullies**, who use words to hurt their **victims**. There are **physical bullies**, who use their bodies to hurt others. There are bullies who convince others to leave a person out of activities or groups. There are also online bullies, or cyberbullies, who use **technology** to bully. One in three kids have experienced some form of online bullying.

What Is Online Bullying?

Online bullies can use e-mail, instant messaging, texting, or social-networking sites to bully their victims. Online bullying is one of the hardest kinds of bullying to spot since the bully and the victim do not need to be near each other. It can also be hard to stop since schools often cannot get involved when it happens away from school grounds.

A bully might think that because he is not physically hurting his victim that he cannot get in trouble for what he is doing.

A bully might text a series of mean messages to try to hurt a victim's feelings or to make her feel scared.

Sometimes online bullies use technology to get back at people who bully them in school. Other times people think it is funny or like the feeling of power they get when bullying online. No matter why someone bullies, it is always wrong.

The Effects of Bullying

Online bullying has both short-term and long-term effects. In the short term, bullied kids may seem sad or **depressed**. They may withdraw from friends and activities. Fear and **anxiety** can cause grades to drop and the victim may fall behind in school. The feelings of fear, anger, and depression can be with the victim long after the bullying stops.

Being bullied might make a victim feel angry because she feels like no one is helping her make the bully stop.

A kid who is already shy might become even more withdrawn if bullies are picking on him.

The effects of online bullying can often be seen more quickly than they can with other forms of bullying. This is because the victim cannot get away from the bully. Online bullying can happen at any time of the day, seven days a week!

Don't Engage the Bully

When a person is bullied in the schoolyard, an **assertive** response can sometimes stop the attacks. However, in online bullying, it is better to ignore the bully. A response might open you up to worse bullying. For example, the bully might use your response to make it seem like you are the bully and get you into trouble. He might also use your response to bully you further.

If you forward a bully's messages to a victim to other friends, you are becoming part of the cycle of bullying yourself.

It is tempting to send a bully a mean message right back. This lets the bully know that she has gotten a reaction out of you, though.

Even if you are not the victim, you should ignore e-mails, texts, and instant messages that target another person. Do not forward them to other friends. This encourages the bully and makes things worse for the victim.

Protect Yourself

If someone is using online media to bully you, there are ways you can **protect** yourself. It is important to save or take screen shots of instant messages or e-mails from a bully. Then block the sender of the hurtful or threatening communications.

Check the **privacy** settings on your computer, or have a parent help you. It can help to **restrict** the people who can send you messages to a preapproved list. It also helps if you keep your "buddy lists" private. This way a bully will not know when you are online.

If you are being cyberbullied, keep the e-mails and save screen shots so that you will have evidence of the bullying to show to a parent, teacher, or other trusted adult.

Talk to an Adult

Many victims do not tell anyone that they are being bullied. They are embarrassed or feel like nobody can help them. Not talking just lets the bullying continue, though.

A parent can help you come up with a plan to deal with online bullying. She can also talk with you about how bullying is making you feel.

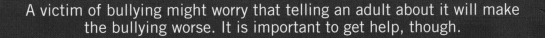
A victim of bullying might worry that telling an adult about it will make the bullying worse. It is important to get help, though.

If you are being bullied at school or online, you should talk to a trusted adult about the bullying. They can listen to how you are feeling and help you deal with those feelings. They can also help you think of ways to put a stop to the bullying. The bullying may not stop overnight, but you will feel stronger knowing you have an ally and that things will get better.

Report Online Bullying

One thing an adult might tell you to do to stop a cyberbully is to report it. This means reporting abuse to the bully's phone or Internet provider. Some providers have a button you can press to report a sender. If someone using an instant-messaging service gets "warned" or "notified" enough times, the provider will shut down the account.

Reporting abuse is one way to stop online bullying. This is why it is important to save, copy, or track the messages you receive.

If a bully is targeting you through a website, look for a button that lets you report abuse. Bullying is against the terms of service, or rules, of most websites.

   If there is not a special button to report abuse, you can go to the provider's website and click on Contact Us and send a description of the abuse. If an online bully threatens to hurt you, report this kind of abuse to the police.

Repairing Your Self-Esteem

The victim of a bully may have low **self-esteem** after days and weeks of being harassed. Sometimes bullies target people who have low self-esteem to begin with. Can you imagine what happens to that person's feelings of self-worth after being bullied?

A teacher, counselor, parent, and other trusted adult are all good people to talk to about how bullying has affected you.

Taking part in charity or volunteer activities can build your self-esteem because you are doing something positive.

It is important to remember that bullying is wrong and that it is not your fault. If you are having trouble dealing with feelings of sadness or anger, you may want to speak with a **counselor**. Counselors are good at helping people understand and deal with difficult feelings so they can move past them.

Technology Is a Tool

Technology is an important tool. People have access to more information than ever before. They can check the weather, text a parent that practice is cancelled, and do research for a science paper all from their cell phones.

Learning how to use technology is more than just learning about different programs and apps. You also need to learn about online safety and privacy.

You may think it is annoying when a parent wants to know who you are talking to and what you are doing online. She is just trying to keep you safe, though!

Despite all the amazing things we can do with our computers, phones, and other technology, we should never use these tools as weapons to hurt others. If someone is using them to hurt you or someone you know, you should tell an adult. We want to use technology for all the wonderful ways it can help us but never to hurt others.

Showing Respect Online

No one deserves to be bullied. It does not matter what people look or act like. We do not have to be friends with everyone, but we do need to treat others with **respect**.

If you are being bullied online, remember not to respond and to save or copy the message and block the sender. If the attacks continue, it is time to get some help. Stay strong and remember that the bullying is not your fault!

Computers are tools that can be used for learning and entertainment. You should never use them as tools to hurt someone's feelings even if you are angry or do not like that person.

Glossary

anxiety (ang-ZY-eh-tee) Uneasiness or worry.

assertive (uh-SER-tiv) Being firm in a positive way.

counselor (KOWN-seh-ler) Someone who talks with people about their feelings and problems.

depressed (dih-PRESD) Having a sickness in which a person is very sad for a long time.

humiliates (hyoo-MIH-lee-ayts) Makes someone else feel very bad about himself or herself.

physical bullies (FIH-zih-kul BU-leez) People who use their bodies to hurt others.

privacy (PRY-vuh-see) The freedom to be alone and not watched.

protect (pruh-TEKT) To keep safe.

respect (rih-SPEKT) Thinking highly of someone or something.

restrict (rih-STRIKT) To keep within limits.

self-esteem (self-uh-STEEM) Happiness with oneself.

taunts (TONTS) Makes fun of someone else or hurts his or her feelings.

technology (tek-NAH-luh-jee) Advanced tools that help people do and make things.

verbal bullies (VER-bul BU-leez) People who use words to hurt other people.

victims (VIK-timz) People or animals that are harmed or killed.

Index

Websites

Due to the changing nature of Internet links, PowerKids Press has developed an online list of websites related to the subject of this book. This site is updated regularly. Please use this link to access the list:
www.powerkidslinks.com/subp/online/